Living Theosis:

Theosis as the Heart of the Cappadocian Home

Living Theosis

Theosis as the Heart of the Cappadocian Home

Veronia Saad

AGORA
UNIVERSITY
PRESS
EST. 2012

Living Theosis: Theosis as the Heart of the Cappadocian Home

Copyright © 2021 by Agora University Press

All rights reserved. Printed in the United States of America. No part of this book may be used or reproduced in any manner whatsoever without written permission except in the case of brief quotations embodied in critical articles or reviews.

For more information, contact: aupress@agora.ac

Agora University Press: press.agora.ac

ISBN 978-1-950831-36-4 (print)
    978-1-950831-37-1 (e-book)

Printed in the United States of America

HIS HOLINESS POPE TAWADROS II
118th Pope and Patriarch of the great city of Alexandria and the See of St. Mark.

HIS HOLINESS PATRIARCH IGNATIUS APHREM II
Patriarch of Antioch and All the East.

Table of Contents

Introduction 6

Chapter 1: Who Were the Cappadocian Mothers? 11
    St. Macrina the Elder.................12
    St. Emmelia..........................13
    St. Macrina the Younger............14
    St. Nonna............................16
    St. Gorgonia.........................18

Chapter 2: The Church in the Home........20
    Motherhood..........................20
    Virtue: Education of the Heart.....26
    Virtue of Parenting..................28
    Virtue of Teaching..................29
    Virtue of Prayer and Marriage.....30
    Virtue of Hospitality...............31
    Education of the Mind..............32

Chapter 3: Our Contemporary Problem....37
    The Problem........................37
    Why We Have This Problem.......39
    Secular 1............................39
    Secular 2............................40
    Secular 3............................42
    This Generation's Aching Heart...47
    A Failure in the Life of Virtue....48
    A Higher Calling....................49

Chapter 4: The Solution……………………....52
    What is the Role of the Church?...52
        Culture…………………………..56
        Discipleship…………………….57

Conclusion...62
Bibliography...65

Introduction

We live in an age that is constantly bombarding us with information. We are a generation that thrives off of knowledge; it seems almost that we are aiming towards knowing all the answers to every question that we could possibly ever ask. Whatever society does, the church seems to be unconsciously imitating. From a young age, during our time at church, we are constantly being feed information so that one day we will know the answers as to why we hold certain rituals and practices in our church communities. In turn, that often creates a mindset that church is for acquiring information about the all-powerful God whom we should be worshiping. We try and do what we can to bring young people into the church to feed them with more information, in response to the hungry minds. We have been tricked to think that our young people's desires, or even our own, is to have as much knowledge about the church as possible because after all, that is the only thing that will keep them inside the church. They are less likely to stray away and attend elsewhere or, God forbid, not be interested in the church at all. The world around us offers entertainment and by extension, we also feel we have to do the same as a church, to keep our people engaged in church, to convince them that our product is the best out there. Yet despite all our best efforts to engage young people in the church, they just simply seem interested. Has the world become so flat that there is less care for the transcendent or are we doing something wrong as a church? Are young people disengaged because they simply do not care or have no interest in church or their Creator? Rodney Stark in his book *Triumph of Faith*,[1] argues quite the opposite; now, more than ever, this generation longs for that which satisfies the soul, it seeks to know and find the Divine. Whoever the Divine may be, young people are on a quest of their own to fulfill their thirst for the mysterious.

The Barna Group illustrated that sixty percent of young people fall away from the church.[2] As a response to this the department of Youth and Young Adults in the Greek Orthodox Archdiocese of North America conducted a four-year study to find out why and how the church can prevent this from happening.[3] It is almost ironic; now, more than ever, local churches hold various events, retreats, and ministries to cater to the congregation. The fruit of all these activities seems to be a sixty percent *decrease* of engagement from young people. Their experience is marked by disconnection and isolation from the church. I argue that the Greek Orthodox Church is not an isolated case of this occurrence. What is striking are the cries in peoples' heart, who long to belong and connect with the church. They battle through depression, anxiety, and pain all on their own. Church is no longer a place of safety, no longer a place to

---

[1] Rodney Stark, *The Triumph of Faith: Why the World Is More Religious than Ever*, (Wilmington: Intercollegiate Studies Institute, 2015).
[2] "Church Dropouts Have Risen to 64%—But What About Those Who Stay?," *Barna Group*, accessed December 8, 2020, https://www.barna.com/research/resilient-disciples/.
[3] "Effective Christian Ministry," *Effective Christian Ministry*, accessed September 17, 2020, https://effectivechristianministry.org/.

belong, to be known and to be loved. It is not that they neither care for the church nor lack interest but it is that they *long* for the church. They long for their Beloved and they long so badly to be part of the Body of Christ. Talking with young adults who have fallen away from the church, the Greek Orthodox Church found that despite being plugged into all the mid-week youth meetings and Sunday school, once one graduated high school almost instantly one was no longer involved.[4] There are countless stories of the poster child who would faithfully attend church but then, a sudden switch followed when they move on to college. The study came to the realization that what the church fails to do is to attach the young parishioners to Christ. Instead, the church attaches them to ministries and youth groups.[5] No wonder they do not feel like they belong to the Body of Christ; these young people belonged to Friday night youth meetings, to Sunday School, to Bible studies, and to young adult group.

Their commitment was to these programs and not a commitment to their Mother, the Church.

In this work, I explore the solution this problem in how our homes and our local parishes can be a place of transformation for its people rather than a place of information. I will be doing so by looking at the Cappadocian Mothers who illustrated a Christocentric home-church in the fourth century, as recounted in the works of the Cappadocian Fathers. Their model of a life of holiness and virtue created homes of transformation which led to the

---

[4] *Ibid.*
[5] *Ibid*, Module I.

deep theology of the famous Cappadocian Fathers that we know today: St. Basil the Great, St. Gregory of Nyssa and St. Gregory the Theologian.

I will begin by addressing who the Cappadocian Mothers were and how we have come to know of them despite having no record of their own writings. Through the writings of the Cappadocian Fathers, we see the great influence these women had on them, how these women shaped the theology that these great heroes of the faith passed on. In the second chapter, I examine the works of St. Basil, St. Gregory of Nyssa, and St. Gregory the Theologian where they speak very highly of their grandmothers, mothers and sister: St. Macrina the Elder, St. Emmelia, St. Nonna, St. Macrina the Younger, and St. Gorgonia. Their writings were shaped by the Christocentric households that these women nurtured, and I show how this was manifested. Chapter three will present what our contemporary challenges are that prevent us from Christ-centered living in our homes and parishes; how we as Orthodox Christians fail our children when we do not know the aches of their hearts and we respond to them with the wrong solution. Finally, I highlight the purpose of mankind and question myself whether or not our homes and church ministries reflect such a purpose in the fourth chapter. I propose that it is through the ministry of discipleship, as shown by the Cappadocians, do we inherit the faith that has been preserved for us by the Church. It is through discipleship that one is able to imitate the ways of Christ that fulfills the goal of mankind. The last commands Christ gives his disciples on earth is in Matthew 28:19: "go therefore and make disciples of all nations...teaching them to obey everything I have commanded you."

Chapter 1
Who were the Cappadocian Mothers?

"You know the woman by the house she makes. Some homes have always a somber air. Some people's religion seems to make them severe and ungentle. But that is not the Christian way. The religion which the word of Christ inspires is sunny and songful."
Royal Martyr Empress Alexandra

The Cappadocian mothers were the great women behind the great men that we know today as the Cappadocian Fathers: Basil the Great, Gregory of Nyssa, and Gregory the Theologian. These virtuous women personified theology to these men.[6] Sunberg boldly proclaims that it is "impossible to separate the women from their [Cappadocian fathers'] theology or their theology from the women."[7] The development of the fathers' theology was made possible because of the women's "environments that allowed them to flourish to the greatest extent of their potential resulted in the three Cappadocian fathers who would forever be remembered as defenders of Nicene Orthodoxy."[8]

---

[6] C.D. Sunberg and T.A. Noble, *The Cappadocian Mothers* (Eugene: Wipf and Stock, 2017), 21.
[7] *Ibid*, 16.
[8] *Ibid*, 115.

In this first chapter, I highlight five extraordinary women who nurtured and taught these great fathers of the Church, who in turn informed our teachings and doctrines that have been preserved for us until today. These women's lives and examples shine a light to how our homes and local parishes today should look like. Their model puts into question how far we are from the life that they lived.

St. Macrina the Elder

St. Macrina the Elder leads the introduction of the women behind the great men. This great saint, in my opinion, is the one who molded the Cappadocian Fathers into who they are by exemplifying a life committed to her Creator. Born in AD 270, she lived out the legacy passed down to her from the Apostles through her father St. Gregory Thaumaturgis.[9] Thaumaturgis, entered a completely pagan region, which Macrina was a part of, but he left this region, Pontus, completely Christian through his inspiration and encouragement. There is little that is known about Macrina, but it was through her preserving the teachings and life-giving spirit, that we have the theology that Basil the Great and Gregory of Nyssa later developed.[10]

What we know is that Macrina and her husband lived an affluent life until they were forced to flee their home in Pontus where for seven years they relied on the provisions

---

[9] Roy J. Deferrari, *Saint Basil: The Letters* (Cambridge: Harvard University Press, 1961), 168 – 9.
[10] "St. Macrina the Elder," *Catholic Encyclopedia*, accessed July 4, 2020, https://www.newadvent.org/cathen/09508b.htm.

of God as they hunted and took shelter in the forests.[11] Their son, Basil the Elder (Macrina the Younger's father), was an only child who became the husband of Emmelia, the mother of saints.

St. Emmelia

St. Emmelia, the mother of saints, was married Basil the Elder who was the son of Macrina the Elder. This couple lived a life of harmony with the Church and their Savior. The life of Christ echoed throughout their home which cultivated four saints from their children, three bishops, and ascetical communities being built in their family estate. The family lived in Pontus with their nine children, Macrina the Younger being the eldest, and Peter of Sebaste being the youngest. After the death of Basil the Elder, Macrina the Younger encouraged Emmelia to live a life of celibacy and to start an ascetic community. Our knowledge of Emmelia mainly comes to us through Gregory of Nazianzen, who was a good friend to Basil the Great and would often be at their home. Nazianzen exclaims at Basil's eulogy:

> "who has not known Emmelia, whose name was a forecast of what she became, or else whose life was an exemplification of her name? For she had a right to the name which implies gracefulness, and occupied, to speak

---

[11] Gregory Nazianzen, "Oration 43," *New Advent*, accessed July 4, 2020, https://www.newadvent.org/fathers/310243.htm.

concisely, the same place among women, as her husband among men."[12]

Truly her name was a reflection of who she was as the name Emmelia in Greek means in tune, well-timed, harmonious, melodious; and generally, regular, agreeable, elegant, graceful.[13] A true indication on the type of woman Emmelia was is echoed in her final breathe as she prayed:

> "To Thee, O Lord, I dedicate the first-fruit and the tenth of the fruits of my womb. My first fruit is this my first-born daughter, and the tenth is my last-born son. According to the Law of Moses, the first fruit and the tenth of the fruits are offered and hallowed to Thee. Therefore, let Thy sanctification and grace come upon this first-fruit and upon my tenth."[14]

St. Macrina the Younger

Emmelia's first born, Macrina the Younger, was the teacher to her mother and siblings, the one who "drew [them] with such speed towards the goal of philosophy,"[15] becoming a spiritual leader to many. She was born in AD

---

[12] Ibid.
[13] Henry George Liddell, Robert Scott, and Roderick McKenzie, *Greek-English Lexicon, Ninth Edition with a Revised Supplement*, ed. Henry Stuart Jones (Oxford: Clarendon Press, 1996), 218
[14] Holy Apostles Convent and Dormition Skete Icons, *The Lives of the Spiritual Mothers*, (Buena Vista: Holy Apostles Convent Publications, 1993), 191.
[15] Gregory of Nyssa, "The Life of Macrina," *Monastic Matrix,* accessed July 7, 2020, https://monasticmatrix.osu.edu/cartularium/life-macrina-gregory-bishop-nyssa.

327. Macrina was not formally schooled, like her brothers, but profoundly knew and lived the Scriptures. Through Macrina, the Cappadocian Fathers were able to develop the teaching of deification and Christianized the pagan word *theosis* to mean so.[16]

By Macrina's profound relationship with the Word, she began the Annisa community which consisted of unceasing prayers with the singing of the Scriptures.[17] The pillars of the community were labor work, hospitality, and physical service for those in need in the local area.[18] Her way of being was a life solely dedicated to her Beloved bridegroom, which outpoured to all those who came in contact with her. She inspired her younger brothers', both Basil the Great and Gregory of Nyssa, writings that they are moved to dedicate manuscripts after her. We see this in the two main works of *The Life of Macrina* and *On the Soul and Resurrection* by Gregory of Nyssa. These pieces truly reveal to their readers the great philosopher and mentor Macrina was.

A notable story reflecting the life Macrina emulated was told powerfully by her brother Gregory of Nyssa, as he mournfully buried her. It is a story that is still read today in *The Life of Macrina*. Nyssa hurriedly beckons Macrina's call as she writes to him encouraging him to visit her. He arrives to Annisa from Cappadocia and sees that her healthy has

---

[16] Sunberg and Noble, Ibid., 63.
[17] Anna Silvas, *Macrina the Younger: Philosopher of God* (Turnhout: Brepols, 2008).
[18] Gregory of Nyssa, "The Life of Macrina," *Monastic Matrix,* accessed July 7, 2020, https://monasticmatrix.osu.edu/cartularium/life-macrina-gregory-bishop-nyssa.

severely declined. Within a short time of Gregory's visit, Macrina passes away and he is left to arrange her burial. As he beholds her dead body, he notices a scar on her breast. Macrina's servant explains to him that the scar in which she bears is the place where illness was found in Macrina. Macrina, at the time, refused to see a physician and so she stayed up begging the Lord to touch her and heal her. The Lord heard her cry and she was healed but what was left in place was a scar, a reminder of her Beloved.[19] Macrina's scar represents her story, her desire for her Lover, her journey to eternity. As Burrus contemplates, "God writes on Macrina, and Macrina submits."[20]

St. Nonna

This genuine woman of prayer was born in AD 304. She devoted her life as a wife and a mother, mothering the very well-known theologian, Gregory of Nazianzus. Nonna was a fervent and faithful, prayerful woman who never wavered in her faith. She never failed in her prayer life being constantly on her knees for her husband and children. Her husband was pagan at the time of their marriage and it was through her enduring prayers that she brought her dear husband back home to the Christian faith. Her prayers not only saved her husband but also the life of her son. Nazianzus tells us that he was once in the depth of despair, crying out to the Lord

---

[19] Ibid.
[20] Virginia Burrus, "Macrina's Tattoo," *Journal of Medieval and Early Modern Studies* 33, no. 3 (September 1, 2003): 403–17, https://doi.org/10.1215/10829636-33-3-403.

that he may save him from a severe storm at sea. Nonna, having favor in God's eyes, prayed ferociously for her son's dismay and victoriously her prayers physically moved the ship safe to shore.[21]

Nonna lived through many sorrows but prayer was always her weapon even in death, as she passed away while praying in the temple. Nazianzus paints the picture when he narrates,

> "one woman is famed for her domestic labors, another for her grace and chastity, another for her pious deeds and the pains she inflicts on her body, her tears, her prayers, and her charity; but Nonna is renowned for everything, and, if we may call this death, she died while praying."[22]

Nonna's story leaves us with such awe and wonder as we read through the words attributed to her by her son in his oration at her funeral. With such reverence Nazianzus looked up to his parents sharing, "he is the ornament of men, she of women, and not only the ornament but the pattern of virtue."[23] Nazianzus honored his mother so much and took her as this ornament of virtue that is reflected in his fifty epigrams which he wrote after her death.[24] He saw her as

---

[21] Brian Daley, *Gregory of Nazianzus*, (London: Routledge, 2006), 6.
[22] Gregory Nazianzen, "Oration 8," *New Advent*, accessed July 7, 2020, https://www.newadvent.org/fathers/310208.htm. 8.10.
[23] Ibid, 8:5.
[24] Sunberg and Noble, Ibid., 132.

having shared in the "glory of the pious women, Susanna, Mary and the two Annas."[25]

Today in our modern world, Nonna is described as "one of the noblest Christian women of antiquity, [who] exerted a deep and wholesome influence."[26] Her graciousness was seen through her unceasing prayers. She is the one who breathed prayer and is the one who became prayer.

St. Gorgonia

Nonna had another child, Gorgonia, who was a beloved sister to Nazianzus. Gorgonia was another woman that shaped and had an immense impact on Nazianzus. She lived a life of piety and beauty as he contemplates that "her nobility consisted in the preservation of the Image, and the perfect likeness to the Archetype."[27]

Gorgonia was a product of the life of her parents as she too led her own family to the heavenly Jerusalem. Her brother poetically writes,

> "for though she had entered upon a carnal union, she was not therefore separated from the spirit, nor, because her husband was her head, did she ignore her first Head: But what

---

[25] W. R. Paton, trans., *The Greek Anthology, Volume II: Book 7: Sepulchral Epigrams. Book 8: The Epigrams of St. Gregory the Theologian* (London: Harvard University Press, 1917), Epigram 28.

[26] Philip Schaff, *Schaff's History of the Christian Church, Volume 1 Apostolic Christianity A.D. 1-100* (Peabody: Hendrickson Publishers, 1996), 910-1.

[27] Gregory Nazianzen, "Oration 8," *New Advent*, accessed July 7, 2020, https://www.newadvent.org/fathers/310208.htm., 8.6.

is most excellent and honorable, she also won over her husband to her side, and made of him a good fellow-servant, instead of an unreasonable master."[28]

---

[28] Gregory Nazianzen, "Oration 8," *New Advent,* accessed July 7, 2020, https://www.newadvent.org/fathers/310208.htm., 8.8.

Chapter 2

The Church in the Home

"No work any man can do for Christ is more important than what he can and should do in his own home. Men have their part - a serious and important part - yet the mother is the real homemaker. It is her sweet life that gives the home its atmosphere. It is through her love that God comes first to her children."

Royal Martyr Empress Alexandra

This chapter highlights the vocation of mothers as illustrated by the Cappadocian Mothers. How did these mothers live out their vocation and how did their homes take shape? What did the home environment look like in which the famous Cappadocian fathers came from? Can these homes be a model for our modern day lives? Furthermore, what is the importance of fostering the church in the home?

Motherhood

St. Nektarios, a 20th century saint, gives mothers the vocation of a teacher, an educator, and the molder of souls. Mothers are responsible for the formation of the mind and heart, through education and spiritual means.[29] Basil conveys the intertwining of these two faculties and the importance of them being developed from infancy:

> "The soul, while it is still easily molded and soft, while it is still like wax that is easily melted and that easily receives the impression of the shapes that are pressed upon it, must straightway and from the beginning be urged on to every exercise of virtues; so that, when the faculty of reason has come and the habit of discrimination has appeared, the soul's course may proceed from first principles and from the impressions of piety that have been handed down to it, with the faculty of reason suggesting that which is useful and the moral character producing an ease of accomplishing it."[30]

It is from infancy that the mother's role comes into play. She is the potter while her child's soul and mind are the clay in her hands, shaping and fashioning their being. The child takes on the mother's image, she is the model for the child through her way of being and becoming. The child imitates both the virtues and the faults of the mother.[31] It is a form of discipleship, mentorship, a rabbi/teacher, to a student. The impressions left in childhood is what is carried on for the rest of their lives, it is stamped into their being and into their identity.

---

[29] St. Nektarios of Pentapolis, *For Mind and Heart: St. Nektarios as Teacher*, Rev Dr John Palmer, trans. (Newrome Press LLC, 2020), 16.
[30] Ibid.
[31] Ibid.

It is the mother's responsibility to awaken those initial desires of God which every human soul longs for. Basil testifies to his mother being the one who instilled and aroused the conceptions of God in him which "I brought to completion the beginnings handed down to me by her."[32] Basil affirms this in a letter where he refutes a certain teaching by Eustathius of Sebasteia, who was once a teacher to Basil, claiming his unwavering teachings that he had received from his childhood.

This same sentiment is echoed by Pestalozzi, a great modern educator, as he declared,

> "I believed in my mother. Her heart showed me God. My God is my mother's God. The God of my heart is the God of my mother's heart. Mother, mother! You showed me God in your instructions, and I found Him in my obedience."[33]

The mother's heart guides the child and leads him to his Maker, the One his soul was made for.[34] St. John Chrysostom, in his homily on I Timothy, presents us with the image of a garden. Like the gardener who, from day one of planting his seeds, is constantly uprooting weeds, cultivating the soil and always tending to his garden, so too should mothers be doing the same to their children. He emphasizes the importance how this should begin from

---

[32] Basil the Great, " Letter 223," *New Advent*, accessed August 12, 2020, https://www.newadvent.org/fathers/3202223.htm.
[33] Nektarios, Ibid., 18
[34] Ibid.

infancy, like the gardener, when the child is easier to mold and form and the weeds more manageable.

The appreciation for mothers being a pillar to their children resounds throughout human history. The honorable Napoleon once asked Henriette Campan, a renowned educator, "What does France need in order to acquire good and honorable men?" This woman replied most profoundly, "Mothers." And to this he responded, "then appoint enough such women for this great national purpose."[35] Fifteen centuries prior the Cappadocian mothers were appointed by God to do just that.

The Cappadocian mothers whom we introduced in the first chapter certainly lived out their vocations as mothers, teachers, and educators. They demonstrated homes of piety, holiness, and virtue despite the trying environment of heresies in which they lived.[36] These women led Christocentric homes in which every part of their daily life was a movement towards the heavenly kingdom. In this region of Asia Minor, the women were the front line of a movement that was coined the Domestic Ascetic Movement.[37] This movement took shape as whole families committed their lives to seeking a life of Christian virtue, in this way the women altered the culture by nurturing the chanting of Scriptures and church traditions in the home.[38]

---

[35] Ibid, 19.
[36] "Mitchell, Anatolia: Land, Men, and Gods in Asia Minor – Bryn Mawr Classical Review," accessed August 12, 2020, https://bmcr.brynmawr.edu/1995/1995.02.02/.
[37] Silvas, Ibid.
[38] Ibid.

These homes became the womb for the growth and maturation for our much beloved Cappadocian fathers: Basil the Great, Gregory of Nyssa and Gregory of Nazianzus. The women that surrounded these great men embodied their theology and writings[39] as,

> "these theologians were not necessarily trying to establish something as they were trying to understand and explain what they were personally experiencing."[40]

This personified life illustrates a tangible manifestation of the spiritual life which in turn became doctrinal traditions rather than theoretical concepts. There was no duality for the Cappadocian families between life and doctrine.[41] They became "theology by the way of biography."[42] Their *telos* "was to be Christians and be called Christians."[43] And to be called a Christian was to live a life of *theosis*, deification. This theological teaching became the crux of who and what the Fathers wrote. These women, Macrina the Elder, Emmelia, Macrina the Younger, Nonna, and Gorgonia, whose lives we find described in the writings of the Fathers, can be appreciated as the models for part of the Cappadocian's development of the doctrine of deification.[44]

---

[39] Sunberg and Noble, Ibid., 23.
[40] Ibid, 21.
[41] Ibid, 35.
[42] Ibid, 118.
[43] Gregory Nazianzen, "Oration 43," *New Advent*, accessed July 4, 2020, https://www.newadvent.org/fathers/310243.htm.
[44] Sunberg and Noble, Ibid., 116.

The Cappadocian fathers were very much aware of the influence their mothers and sisters had on them and in also who they became. Nazianzen affirms this when he said,

> "I marveled when I looked on Emmelia's offspring, so great and of such kind, all the wealth of her mighty womb! But when I noted that she was Christ's possession, of pious blood, Emmelia, this is what I said: 'No wonder! The root is so great.' This is the holy recompense of your piety, O best of women, the honor of your children, for whom you had but one desire."[45]

Nazianzus marvels at the great root of Basil and Nyssa's family, the illustrious Emmelia as he watches in wonder the great wealth of her womb. Emmelia's graciousness and gentleness, as her name confirms, effects beyond her own household as is witnessed by Nazianzus, who is a close friend to the family.[46]

Nazianzus wonders both at Nyssa's family and his own family as they became such pious families, who shaped our Church today worldwide through the life they lived and the relationships they nurtured. They were patterns of virtue[47] for each other. It was the women, fulfilling their vocation, emphasizing while instilling and fostering a life of virtue. These two families became renowned for their virtue and

---

[45] Paton, Ibid., 162.
[46] Gregory Nazianzen, "Oration 43," *New Advent*, accessed July 4, 2020, https://www.newadvent.org/fathers/310243.htm.
[47] Gregory Nazianzen, "Oration 8," *New Advent*, accessed July 7, 2020, https://www.newadvent.org/fathers/310208.htm.

sainthood.[48] Basil, Nyssa, and Nazianzus all acquired the characteristics that these women displayed in their homes, who shaped the way, through pursing virtue, to a life of *theosis*, union with God.[49] Sunberg describes these women as those who "paved the way, living lives of virtue which became road maps for men and women alike, leading all to the very likeness of Christ."[50] Theosis was infused in their life that the rhythm of virtue developed.

The life of virtue is recalled over and over in the writings we find by these Fathers. What was this life of virtue that they spoke of?

Virtue: Education of the Heart

In the opening chapter of Guroian's book *Tending the Heart of Virtue*, he makes a distinction between values and virtue. Values are what people hold to be of value and importance, something in which they stand for, whereas virtues are part of one's character, it is part of who they are rather than an idea they hold to.[51] Guroian goes on to say that in order to nourish virtuous persons, one needs to be educated through stories. Stories awaken the wonder of a child; they arouse the child's desire to know and to be known by their Maker. Stories awaken the child's soul and hunger to live a life of virtue in order to be able to commune with

---

[48] Sunberg and Noble, Ibid., 149.
[49] Ibid, 207.
[50] Ibid.
[51] Vigen Guroian, *Tending the Heart of Virtue: How Classic Stories Awaken a Child's Moral Imagination*, (New York: Oxford University Press, 2002).

their Creator.[52] To practice virtue is out of a "love of God and Christ" rather than a desiring to become a better moral person.[53]

Basil illustrated this way of storytelling as he mentions his unwavering faith which came from his grandmother, Macrina, who would tell of the stories of her spiritual mentor, St. Gregory the Wonderworker.[54] The way of discipleship was the vehicle which carried the ways of virtue very evidently in the Cappadocians. It was becoming theology by biography,[55] becoming virtue by stories, whether it be stories from the past or stories of their own family members.

Nyssa goes on to document the life of Macrina as an incarnation of virtue, as her only goal is a life with her Beloved.[56] By telling his own sister's story, this illustrates to the reader how this famous Saint honors such a life and wishes others to be inspired and moved to live a life dedicated to Christ. That is what stories do. The idea of discipleship will be discussed more in detail in chapter four.

The goal and purpose of living a life of virtue is to participate in the process of deification, which is the goal of humankind's existence. Deification is the goal of Christian living, to be transformed into the image of God by living a

---

[52] Ibid.
[53] Gregory of Nazianzen, "Oration 18," *New Advent*, accessed August 21, 2020, https://www.newadvent.org/fathers/310218.htm.
[54] Silvas, *Ibid.*, 12-3.
[55] Sunberg and Noble, Ibid., 98.
[56] Gregory of Nyssa, *The Life of Saint Macrina*, trans. Kevin Corrigan (Eugene: Wipf and Stock, 2005).

life of virtue in imitation of Christ, becoming a disciple of Christ. In the words of St. Paul, "Imitate me as I imitate Christ" (I Corinthians 11:1).

Today, through the intercessory help of the Cappadocian Mothers, we can acquire and live out the virtuous life that leads to a participation with the Divine, who in turn fills our lives with an abundance.

Virtue of Parenting

Emmelia, in her virtue of parenting, presents to us an icon of motherhood with having four of her children canonized as saints and deserving of the title as "mother of saints." This is evident by her last words surrounded by two of her children,

> "To you, O Lord, do I offer the first and the tenth fruit of my labor pains. This is my first born, my eldest daughter, and this my tenth child, my last-born son. To you, both have been consecrated by law and your votive offerings they are. So may sanctification come to this my first and to this my tenth born."[57]

Emmelia, as a mother and parent, entrusted her children to their Savior and fostered great wonder in them as Nazianzus exclaimed the marvelous root from which Basil and Nyssa came from.[58]

---

[57] Ibid.
[58] Paton, Ibid.

Virtue of Teaching

Macrina, in her virtue of teaching, became the icon of the Teacher. Nyssa describes her as, "she who had raised herself through philosophy to the highest limit of human virtue."[59] A philosophical life was a life of virtue and, as a good teacher who longs for her students to live this philosophical life, so too did Macrina with her own brother, Basil. When Basil returned from Athens he was "monstrously conceited [in his] skill in rhetoric,"[60] he was "contemptuous of every high reputation and exalted beyond the leading lights of the province by his self-importance."[61] Even to her own mother was Macrina a teacher who through the tragedy of losing her youngest brother, "with her firm, unflinching spirit she taught her mother's [Emmelia] soul to be brave."[62] Macrina was a teacher to the soul, guiding with compassion, wisdom, being the model for her students,

> "she rose above nature and by means of her own reasoned reflections she lifted her mother up together with her and placed her beyond suffering, guiding her to patience and courage by her own example."[63]

---

[59] Gregory of Nyssa, *The Life of Saint Macrina*, 29.
[60] Ibid.
[61] Ibid.
[62] Ibid.
[63] Ibid.

Virtue of Prayer and Marriage

Nonna, in citing her name was an incitement to virtue,[64] was the emblem of both prayer and marriage. Her cultivation in prayer lead her to a become an icon for a Biblical and godly marriage: "she both called her husband lord and regarded him as such."[65] She embraced Christ as her Bridegroom that she was able to honor her husband in the way Christ calls each wife to in marriage. Nonna, in embracing prayer as her life became prayer as is accentuated by Nazianzus in dedicating fifty epigrams on the manner of her death, during prayer, in church.[66] Prayer beautified her soul as she moved towards a restoration of the Divine image.[67] She "stood like a pillar at the night long and daily psalmody."[68]

Nazianzus honors his parent's marriage despite not being married himself and saw them as the most admirable man and woman who were so knit together in love, harmony, and godliness. They "were so united that their marriage was a union of virtue rather than of bodies."[69]

---

[64] Gregory Nazianzen, "Oration 8," *New Advent*, accessed July 7, 2020, https://www.newadvent.org/fathers/310208.htm.
[65] Ibid.
[66] Paton, Ibid., 8.
[67] Gregory of Nazianzen, "Oration 18," *New Advent*, accessed August 21, 2020, https://www.newadvent.org/fathers/310218.htm.
[68] Ibid.
[69] Ibid.

Virtue of Hospitality

Gorgonia, Nazianzus' younger sister, was esteemed for her gift of hospitality, welcoming the stranger. The doors of her heart and home were open to all and she embraced all. Through her gracefulness and nobility in imitating the Archetype she became within herself an abode to the broken, "oftentimes entertained Christ in the person of those whose benefactress she was."[70] Her native land was Jerusalem above as,

> "her nobility consisted in the preservation of the Image…which is produced by reason and virtue and pure desire, ever more and more conforming, in things pertaining to God, to those truly initiated into the heavenly mysteries."[71]

It is in this orientation of her being that allowed her to be illuminated and see with the eyes of her heart the souls of the wounded.

The virtues that these women cultivated and struggled to acquire lead to the illumination of their children's hearts. This philosophical life included the education of the mind, which these women encouraged in the men also. Nineteenth century Saint Theophan echoes this life as "of all holy works, the education of children is the most holy."[72] This

---

[70] Gregory Nazianzen, "Oration 8," *New Advent*, accessed July 7, 2020, https://www.newadvent.org/fathers/310208.htm., 8.6.
[71] Ibid.
[72] Theophan the Recluse and P. E. Gillquist, *Raising Them Right: A Saint's Advice on Raising Children*, Hieromonk S. Rose, trans., (Chesterton: Ancient Faith Publishing, 2005), 84.

holy work is the formation of both the mind and heart, the intellect and the moral. They both require differing means of sculpting since the heart is of the supernatural world and the mind is of the natural world.[73] Above was a clear example of nurturing and forming the heart through the life of virtue. So, then what did molding the mind look like for these women?

Education of the Mind

Emmelia and Nonna were both very intentional in sending their children to Athens, the hotspot of pagan splendor and idolatry. Unmoved by the pagan teachings, their teachers were in awe of how the mothers influenced their foundations of faith:

> "'Alas!' he exclaimed, 'What manner of women there are among the Christians!,' indicating by these words the cause of this failure. 'How truly beautiful! What radiant examples we have before us in these pious mothers! What wondrous images! What wondrous models! Who can deny that it is the mothers who produce great and virtuous men?'"[74]

Many times, in the writings of the Fathers, we see cultural education interwoven with their theological thought; both mind and heart are present. Basil writes a letter to his students addressing the importance of studying Greek literature and how to approach it. He tells them.

---

[73] Nekatrios, Ibid., 21.
[74] Ibid., 23.

> "to be sure, we shall become more intimately acquainted with these precepts in the sacred writings, but it is incumbent upon us, for the present, to trace, as it were, the silhouette of virtue in the pagan authors."[75]

One must care for his body, specifically his mind, in order to grow his soul towards oneness with God. Basil emphasizes this to his students by advising to only give so much care to the body as is beneficial to the soul.[76] Basil encourages his students to be like the bees who look for what is beneficial and leave that which is not profitable. In praising the beauty that can be found in pagan culture, Basil proclaims that "our aim is virtue and so anyone praising and striving for virtue we should receive his words with pleasure!"[77] Basil cites many pagans in this letter as he values the heroes who seek and struggle for virtue rather than the riches of the world. Virtue is that which distinguishes the hero from the coward, the one who gives his all and suffers for the sake of gaining virtue. In the words of Homer,

> "Be virtue your concern, O men, which both swims to shore with the shipwrecked man, and makes him, when he comes naked to the strand, more honored than the prosperous Phaeacians."[78]

---

[75] Basil the Great, "Address to Young Men on the Right Use of Greek Literature," *Tertullian*, accessed August 28, 2020, http://www.tertullian.org/fathers/basil_litterature01.htm., X.
[76] Ibid.
[77] Ibid.
[78] Ibid., V.

These stories inspire and encourage one to seek that which is virtuous in order to know and be known by the Beloved.

A life of virtue is born when the mind sees and is inspired by virtue which then invokes the heart to purse such a life. Basil points to this inspiration claiming that,

> "every man is divided against himself who does not make his life conform to his words, but who says with Euripides, 'The mouth indeed hath sworn, but the heart knows no oath.' Such a man will seek the appearance of virtue rather than the reality. But to seem to be good when one is not so, is, if we are to respect the opinion of Plato at all, the very height of injustice."[79]

Basil so clearly instructs his students that the goal in pursing such education is for the sake of a heart that is transformed into virtue rather than the illusion of the mind having virtue.

We see the same sentiment in regard to pagan literature in Nazianzus' and Nyssa's writings as is observed by Georgia Frank. Frank discerns the frequent similarities in style and expression that are used in these Fathers with Homer's.[80] Frank goes on to say

---

[79] Ibid., VI.
[80] Georgia Frank, "Macrina's Scar: Homeric Allusion and Heroic Identity in Gregory of Nyssa's Life of Macrina," *Journal of Early Christian Studies* 8, no. 4 (December 1, 2000): 511–30, https://doi.org/10.1353/earl.2000.0063.

"that Gregory should incorporate a Homeric scene in the Life of Macrina is not farfetched, if one considers the Homeric quotes and imagery that pepper his letters and homilies."[81]

This is a great picture of how much influence the contemporary culture had an impact on Nazianzus and how much his mind was shaped by where he was. In the same way, "Macrina was molded by books and literature which in turn helped form her mind and heart and lead her to a life of virginity dedicated to the Lord."[82] With mind and heart formed, the Fathers developed as Christian philosophers, teachers, orators and theologians.

Conclusion

Mirroring Nektarios' statement on mothers being the center of a child's formation, Silvas confirms that the fourth century women were a chief example of such a life. The structure of the Christian family household was the center for holiness and virtue.[83] These women lead homes and in turn, their communities in spiritual zeal, communitarian sensibility, and doctrinal allegiance.[84] These were homes whose citizenship was in heaven. As so evidently seen, these women encountered Christ, the Being, and as a result, they were transfigured into His Likeness. For the Cappadocian Fathers growing up in such an environment, theology for

---

[81] Ibid, 520.
[82] Silvas, Ibid., 32.
[83] Ibid, 47.
[84] Ibid.

them was an encounter with the Living God. Theology was life and life was theology; it was who they were and who they were becoming.

The Cappadocian mothers show us the crucial nature of the role of women in today's homes and churches. The church in the home is of utmost significance as it is where life is breathed into the child. The church in the home is where humankind is transformed into his/her calling as a saint. The women work for the joy of the man and children, and the good of her home[85] for the sake of the One who made them.

Let us today, appoint such women for this great purpose to acquire good and honorable men, as without such women there cannot be such men.

---

[85] Nonna Verna Harrison, Basil, and Verna E. F. Harrison, *On The Human Condition: St Basil the Great* (Crestwood: St Vladimirs Seminary Press, 2005), Oration 1.

Chapter 3

Our Contemporary Problem

In this chapter, I will explore today's world, bearing in mind the discussions of the previous chapter on the Cappadocian mothers in cultivating and living a life of virtue. Do we live in Christocentric homes and participate in Christocentric local parishes? I argue otherwise and explore the reasons why. In this chapter, I will discuss what is hindering our homes and parishes from living such virtuous lives.

I will explore contemporary culture that has so impacted both our homes and parishes today and the problem with the framework that we are currently using in order to live as Christians. I attempt to deeply emphasis the significance of knowing the history and contemporary way that society thought and thinks, in order to be able to navigate our lives as believers of the Faith.

The Problem

Today's current societal problem seems to be systemic and perhaps worldwide. For the sake of this analysis, the focus will be on North America, but this issue is not by any means exclusive to North America. The Coptic Orthodox Church enjoys around a fifty year presence in North America; it continues to grow with new waves of immigration. New parishes continue to be established, either to accommodate new immigrates or for the sake of catering to American-born Copts. As we moved from our homeland to a foreign country, we bring our ideas and ways of doing church with us in order to maintain our heritage and roots. We fear to lose our young people in this new land as they are born and raised far from the homeland. This fear drives us to overcompensate by desperately trying to keep the youth of today in church by attracting them to activities, events, and retreats held in their local parishes. Our mindset became one that we must indoctrinate our children in order to not lose them to the world. Yet with the local church's calendar being full, one dares to ask the question of what benefit do these ministries and their activities have for our young people? Is it merely to keep our churches full, to keep our heritage alive, to live in an Egyptian microcosm where we may continue our way of life that we have left behind? I believe our answer lies in the fruit of these activities and events, and also where our young people are today in terms of the Church in the context of the current society. But what does this all mean?

When the Coptic Church moved from Egypt to North America, then inevitably, North American society shaped and continues to shape our young people's minds, which is not necessarily something negative. We lose many young people whom we institutionalized and those who remain are merely observers in the Church life, when we consider the fruit of these ministries. Their observation opposes a way in which one is called in this life, a way of participation in the Life of the Church and therefore, the Life of Christ. The life of an observer does not fulfill one's calling of being transformed into the Likeness of Christ. The observer does not struggle in the ways of virtue in order to participate with the Holy Spirit to obtain *theosis*. So, we currently have a church packed with meetings, events, activities and retreats but barely any transformed disciples of Christ.

Why We Have This Problem

We will begin here on a journey of discovery: why do we have such a problem? We will travel through history in order to be able to appreciate where we are today. I will use three terms to classify the observed eras: pre-modernity, modernity and post-modernity. The terms used are coined by Charles Taylor in his book *Secular Age*: Secular1, Secular2 and Secular3. These terms are thoroughly explained by James K. Smith in his work, *How (Not) to Be Secular*.

Secular1

We begin with the Platonic age, which is the premodern period: Secular1. The world is naturally in order as it has an intelligible essence. This order is discovered by observation but not all of reality can be seen.[86] This age period is where "sacred work" was done by the clergyman on behalf of the world. The "sacred" and "secular" world were distinct from each other in terms of roles, but at the same time supported each other. Also, both roles believed in an enchanted world

---

[86] Michael Paul Gama and Gerald L. Sittser, *Theosis: Patristic Remedy for Evangelical Yearning at the Close of the Modern Age* (Eugene: Wipf and Stock, 2017), 16.

where one can encounter the divine.[87] The word "secular" was used to refer to what was literally from the earth, the material. "Sacred," meanwhile, referred to that which related to the divine.[88] The supernatural world was a reality for all people in the medieval period, the world was infused with the supernatural, with the mystery. A butcher would close up his shop at the end of the working day and then would make his way to church to pray. Human activity was in accordance with nature's rhythms, they were almost one and the same.[89] There was no denial of God; He was everywhere present, and He was moving, and this was man's reality.[90]

Secular2

In the fifteenth century, the Renaissance came knocking at the door with a man-centered mindset.[91] Man had the power as he began to master the world through inventions and as a consequence, a division began to slowly emerge between mankind and nature's rhythms. There became an increased focused on the earthly more than the heavenly.[92] This line of thinking opened the doors for the Reformation which brought in individual thought and experience. Each man became his own authority as Martin Luther lived and

---

[87] James K. A. Smith, *How (Not) to Be Secular: Reading Charles Taylor* (Grand Rapids: Eerdmans, 2014).
[88] "Effective Christian Ministry." Module II, Lesson I.
[89] Richard Tarnas, *The Passion of the Western Mind: Understanding the Ideas That Have Shaped Our World View*, Reprint Edition (New York: Ballantine Books, 1993), 225.
[90] "Effective Christian Ministry." Module II, Lesson I.
[91] Gama and Sitter, Ibid., 17.
[92] Ibid, 18.

preached unless he was convicted by Scripture and plain reason,[93] he would not believe. An individual with his own perception and understanding would determine the interpretation of his faith and of the Holy Scriptures.[94] Rationalism was creeping in as the higher governance.

The Reformation was a steppingstone for the Age of the Enlightenment in the seventeenth century. The Enlightenment reorientated man's focus to a rational and an empirical encounter with the world. The world could now be examined through the material, bereft of God and His transcendence. Gama described this era as disenchanted; the world was no longer filled with wonder and mystery.[95] The human mind increasingly became the control center as it observed, experimented, and measured nature. As a consequence, creation and everything in it was perceived as a machine, very static in nature.[96] The divine was subtracted from the cosmos. Taylor dubs this period Secular2.[97]

The Enlightenment then became the mother of Modernity, a world devoid of its Creator. The hallmarks of Modernity were "autonomous individualism, demystification, secularization, naturalistic reductionism,

---

[93] Martin Luther's speech, "Diet in Worms," https://www.sjsu.edu/people/james.lindahl/courses/Hum1B/s3/Luther-Speech-Worms-1521.pdf, accessed November 19th, 2020.
[94] Gama and Sittser, Ibid., 22.
[95] Ibid., 24.
[96] Ibid., 27.
[97] Charles Taylor, *A Secular Age*, (Cambridge: Harvard University Press, 2007).

and scientific empiricism."[98] Science became the keeper of world view and so human reason and empirical observation replaced the theological doctrine and scriptural revelation as the principal means for comprehending the universe.[99] The Enlightenment coupled with the Reformation equipped every man to be their own authority as experience became what determined truth. With Secular2 having pushed out the sacred from the world and limited it to specific places, like the Church, Secular3 emerges in a post-modern world.

Secular3

Secular3 brought in a very flattened, cold, and harsh world. Yet despite the disenchantment, a void was felt. The transcendent haunts this new generation because of how impersonal the universe became. According to Smith, Secular3 became the Age of Authenticity, where we define for ourselves the truth and meaning of life. [100]

Why is this history with these terms relevant for us today? This is precisely where our problem lies in our homes and local churches. Without having a full grasp on how the culture moves and thinks, we cannot solve today's problem; why, despite the number of ministries, do we lack disciples of Christ? Perhaps we can look at the Evangelical Church today as experiencing what the Orthodox Church is going

---

[98] Thomas C. Oden, *After Modernity...What?* (Grand Rapids: Zondervan Academic, 1992), 48.
[99] Tarnas, Ibid., 286.
[100] Smith, Ibid.

through, since Evangelism dominates American Christianity and inevitably carries significant influence.

The Pew Study illustrated a consistent decline, of which more than a quarter of American adults (28%) have left their childhood faith.[101] The Evangelical Church is experiencing a mass exodus of millennials due to the disparities between the two generations.[102] A tension takes place between the younger generation and the older generation; the older generation seem to be locked in the immanent frame of Secular2, where, as we said above, is the removal of the sacred from the cosmos. This has led to leaders and parents to develop programs and events to try and protect their kids from being exposed to the secular world outside the walls of their homes and churches. The aim is diluted down to: let us keep the young people in the four walls of the church and make sure they do not leave. Our minds think that we must captivate our children with contemporary means of entertainment in order to keep them attracted to church. And so, we see our children as soldiers, preciously seeing their minds as ground we cannot lose.[103] We must bombard our children with information about the church that they may stand firm against the secular schools and universities that they attend. We want to make sure that the kids know the facts about their faith that they may defend it.

---

[101] "U.S. Religious Landscape Survey: Religious Beliefs and Practices," *Pew Research Center's Religion & Public Life Project* (blog), June 1, 2008, https://www.pewforum.org/2008/06/01/u-s-religious-landscape-survey-religious-beliefs-and-practices/.
[102] Gama and Sittser, Ibid., 42–4.
[103] "Effective Christian Ministry." Module II, Lesson 2.

This can be evidently seen in the way most Sunday School curriculums are formed. The *telos* of this ministry seems to be trying to teach the kids as much information as possible and to solidify such facts, we put on competitions to challenge their memorization of the faith. Yet despite our efforts, we continue to see disengaged young people. Our response continues to be more programs and activities.

The problem is that we are coming up with solutions to the problems of the past, not the challenges that we actually face today.[104] What we are now facing is Secular3, a flat world where the transcendent is irrelevant. Andy Root uses Paul's story as an example of Secular2 and Secular3. Saul was a zealous man for Judaism, willing to kill for what he believed. Saul valued and stood for Jewish doctrine and for him, faith is belief.[105] Root explains this a little further,

> "When we say 'faith,' especially in the shadow of Secular2 and the gravitational pull of Secular3, we often mean something like 'commitment.' We may say that faith is trust, but because we are always doubting our experiences of transcendence and divine action, we turned faith into trust that looks like institutional or religious commitment as a way to battle Secular2 […] we know our young people have faith when they stick to their religious commitments, come to church, and articulate what they believe. Commitment next to the gravitational pull of Secular3 has a great advantage; commitment

---

[104] Ibid.
[105] Ibid.

is dependent not on transcendent force but on our willingness."[106]

Saul was committed to his belief as he knew how to articulate what he believed. In the same way, many of our young people are committed to the church and its beliefs. We measure ministry success by their commitment to ministry programs and their willingness to pass down that same way to the generations to come. We want our young people to be able to know information about the church in order to defend the faith at school and work. But the difference between Saul and Paul, is that Paul had an encounter with Christ, he participated with Him on the road to Damascus and his life was transformed.

> "Saul, who had believed his life's meaning was to defend Judaism against pollution, was shocked to find that his life's work, his life's meaning crumbled before the face of Christ when we met Him on the road."[107]

Faith was transformed from being something to defend and be committed to, to "actually [entering] into Christ; to have our own being taken into the being of Jesus."[108] Paul proclaims in Galatians 2:20 that, "it is no longer I who live, but Christ who lives in me." It is no longer a zealous enthusiasm or event planning or strategies but a *kenosis* that one may be filled with Christ.

---

[106] Andrew Root, *Faith Formation in a Secular Age: Responding to the Church's Obsession with Youthfulness* (Grand Rapids: Baker Academic, 2017), 123–4.
[107] "Effective Christian Ministry." Module II, Lesson 2.
[108] Root, Ibid., 120.

We strive towards the wrong goal in our churches today. We have created "church members to be consumers, [and now] the monster had been created...it demanded to be fed."[109] We have birthed a congregation of spiritual consumers, grown fat and lazy on a continuous diet of quasi-spiritual junk food,[110] with the constant events and activities we continue to host. Our consumers no longer see the value of the product that we are giving them and so naturally our consumers will drift off elsewhere to a more attractive product. Carlson and Lueken challenge us today to prove that this demanding monster exists by descaling the number of services in our churches for three months in order to pray and focus more on Scripture reading.[111] How would the congregation respond? Would our consumers remain part of that church or would they take their business elsewhere?[112]

This Generation's Aching Heart

Secular3, our post-modern world, is a relative world, where experience shapes our individual reality and where we determine our own truth and identity. The vast vacuum that Secular2 left for transcendence causes a longing ache for the mystery and the divine in today's age. Secular2 became about information, whereas our young people today long for

---

[109] Kent Carlson, Mike Lueken, and Dallas Willard, *Renovation of the Church: What Happens When a Seeker Church Discovers Spiritual Formation* (Downers Grove: IVP Books, 2011), 24.
[110] Gama and Sittser, Ibid., 61.
[111] Carlson, Lueken, and Willard, Ibid., 85.
[112] Ibid.

transformation.[113] Modern humanity's appetites have left them gorged on materialism and yearning for spiritual substance.[114] This tells us that we have striped Christ from His Church as our young people long for His healing hand. According to the Pew Study, a quarter of Americans consider themselves to be deeply religious, yet they avoid any affiliation with any church.[115] The dawn of the New Age, is what Ferguson calls this time, the transition from Secular2 to Secular3 is expressed universally in politics, economics, technology, art and music.[116] The New Age makes the current generation crave for genuine spirituality, the longing to know God rather than knowing about Him.[117] Leonard Sweet proposes that,

> "Western Christianity went to sleep in a modern world governed by the gods of reason and observation. It is awakening to a postmodern world open to revelation and hungry for experience. Indeed, one of the last places that the postmodern world expects to be 'spiritual' is the church."[118]

In a popular millennial blog, Rachel Evens, as a response to many others writing about why they left the

---

[113] Gama and Sittser, Ibid., 79.
[114] Ibid., 82.
[115] "More Americans Now Say They're Spiritual but Not Religious," *Pew Research Center* (blog), accessed September 23, 2020, https://www.pewresearch.org/fact-tank/2017/09/06/more-americans-now-say-theyre-spiritual-but-not-religious/.
[116] Marilyn Ferguson, *The Aquarian Conspiracy: Personal and Social Transformation in Our Time*, (New York: TarcherPerigee, 2009), 18-9.
[117] Gama and Sittser, *Ibid.*, 86.
[118] Leonard Sweet, *Post-Modern Pilgrims: First Century Passion for the 21st Century World* (Nashville: B&H Books, 2000), 28.

church, writes as one of her reasons: "we long for Jesus."[119] Is that not a staggering statement to make for reasons leaving the church? I beg to differ that one would find a different response in our Coptic Churches today. Our leaders are on one planet, while our young people are elsewhere. Contemporary literature, the news, social media are all crying out for transformation as self-help becomes today's new religious order. On the other hand, it seems that the Evangelical Church today is laser-focused on outsiders making a one-time decision to accept Jesus, while completely distorting the Gospel, as the Gospel calls us to a life of discipleship rather than a one-time, dramatic decision that needs to be made.[120] Such an obsession yielded in a loss of fifty percent of those who made this decision.[121] In the same way, one can argue that in the Coptic Church, we have become obsessed with getting people to make a commitment to the weekly ministries and programs, and in doing so, we fail to carry out the true calling of the Gospel.

A Failure in the Life of Virtue

Chapter two posited that the Cappadocian Mothers' orientation of their hearts and homes was towards union with God. The *telos* of everything they did in their homes and their local communities was growing into the likeness of the

---

[119] "15 Reasons I Left Church," Rachel Held Evans, accessed September 23, 2020, https://rachelheldevans.com/blog/15-reasons-i-left-church.
[120] Scot McKnight and N. T. Wright and Dallas Willard, *The King Jesus Gospel: The Original Good News Revisited*, Revised Edition (Grand Rapids: Zondervan, 2016), 18.
[121] Ibid., 20.

Image. A virtuous life is one of pain, struggle, and strife. Yet is this the mode in which we operate in our homes and churches today? Do we long for our children to purse a holy life and an encounter with Christ? Are our programs and ministries geared towards our children having enlightened hearts? Do our children know who they are and whose they are, as they agonize over their identity in this New Age?

We have become a church of "doing" rather than a church of "being." We fail our own personhood as we remain in the imminent frame of machinery, where we do not live a dynamic life moving towards the Being who calls us to become.

A Higher Calling

In our culture today, we long for our children to be the best doctors and lawyers, the most well-behaved and polite kids they can be. But our desire for them remains just there; we lack a higher calling for them. "We want them to be just religious enough to keep them out of trouble, but not religious enough to get them into trouble."[122] Our ministries fail to open the hearts of our children that they might encounter the Crucified and Risen Christ, who is the One who calls them into communion. In our Orthodox culture today, we love telling and knowing stories of the great heroes of our Faith who gave their lives for the sake of their Beloved, those who struggled in the Way through pursing virtue. They lived uncomfortably for the sake of a higher

---

[122] "Effective Christian Ministry." Module II, Lesson 2.

calling, for the sake of the Kingdom to come. Their vision was beyond the earthly realm. But because of the Secular3 lens in which we operate, we esteem them because of how profoundly they stood for their beliefs, rather than looking at them as those who encountered Christ Who pursues to transform His flock. Our young people perhaps see them today as heroes because of the values they stood for rather than the virtues they cultivated and sought after. We esteem our modern-day heroes for their courage and commitment towards just causes rather than those who inspire us to grow in character and to see that which is good, beautiful, and true.

Conclusion

Our ministries are not struggling because our young people are not equipped with the right information. This is a Secular2 attitude towards ministry which asserts the taking over of young people's minds so that they may be convinced of the church. Ministry seems to be about getting the kids on our side of the secular-sacred debate rather than a true encounter with the One whom they are truly seeking. As parents and leaders, we need to be asking ourselves why are we continually seek how to keep our children at church? It seems we are losing our children just as much as the Evangelical Church, and we employ the same framework for ministry. We fail to remember what it means to be a Christian and to be called a Christian. We fail to know our kids and to truly know their aching hearts. We continue to give our young people a falsified form of Christianity that does not offer a transformation into the Likeness of Christ.

If our homes fail to carve the church in its heart, then our local churches fail to be churches. As such was the Cappadocian model; the home was the loci of the Christian community. The Cappadocian Fathers reveal in their writings that the goal of our Christian life is *theosis*, which should then be the goal of our homes and in turn, the goal of our ministries. We are failing in our homes and in our churches as we fail to meet the needs of our children and even our own needs.

In the next chapter, we will explore *theosis*, the goal of mankind, which in turn, should be the goal of both our homes and our parishes.

Chapter 4

The Solution

The previous chapter expounded the contemporary challenge that we face today. In this chapter, I discuss the role of the local parish and how it should look based on the definition of the church. I will analyze whether or not the local parish fulfills the fullness of what and who the church is. And so to ask the question, do our ministries reflect this *telos*, this true reality of the Church? I will then suggest ways in which this can be the actuality of our ministries and local parishes.

What is the role of the Church?

Cyprian of Carthage simply defines the role of the earthly church as conveying life to her people through her communion with the Triumphant Church.[123] She conveys this life by safeguarding what she has inherited.[124] The incarnation revealed the heavenly Church through Christ's establishment of the church here on earth.[125] The Eucharist reveals to the people their true reality, the mystery, which is the communion of God and humanity. Through the

---

[123] St Cyprian of Carthage and Allen Brent, *On the Church: Select Treatises,* (Crestwood: St. Vladimir's Seminary Press, 2006), 141.
[124] Cyprian and Allen Brent, *On the Church: Select Letters*, (Crestwood: St. Vladimir's Seminary Press, 2006), 185.
[125] Ibid, 178.

Eucharist, the Church is the fullness of the kingdom proclaimed and manifested in the Body of Christ as we experience it in the community.[126]

This communion of God and humanity is the process of *theosis*, which is the core of the ancient church. The church's objective is the deification of each member.[127] Here there appears to be a parallel between postmodern ideologies identified in chapter three and that of Orthodox Christianity: they both echo a process. A journey which one needs to embark on, a progression one needs to embrace in order to fulfill one's calling.[128] On this journey of deification, one

> "discovers God through the beauty and order of things seen, using sight as a guide to what transcends sight without losing God through the grandeur of what it sees."[129]

Life then becomes a pursuit of constant transformation from "glory to glory" (II Corinthians 3:18). The Psalmist calls us in Psalm 82:6, and proclaims that "you are gods, sons of the Most high, all of you." Centuries later, Clement of Alexandria declares the same sentiment of deification as the purpose of mankind.[130] Man becomes god through his

---

[126] Boris Bobrinskoy, *The Mystery of the Church: A Course in Orthodox Dogmatic Theology*, (Yonkers: St. Vladimir's Seminary Press, 2012), 79.
[127] Gama and Sittser, Ibid., 100.
[128] Gama and Sittser, Ibid., 101.
[129] St Gregory of Nazianzus, *On God and Christ: The Five Theological Orations and Two Letters to Cledonius* (Crestwood: St Vladimirs Seminary Press, 2002), 47.
[130] Clement of Alexandria, "The Paedagogus," *New Advent*, accessed May 17, 2019, http://www.newadvent.org/fathers/02091.htm.

participation in the Holiness of God since this is the fulfillment of man.[131]

Theosis then becomes humanity's purpose as it is the response to the Incarnate Word of God. Gregory of Nazianzus tells us to "…become as Christ is, since Christ became as we are."[132] *Theosis* becomes the process in which we become fully human.[133]

Theosis is the vocation of humanity, which is realized in a personal encounter with God, a face-to-face encounter. This initiative is by God Himself, who reaches out to us through the Incarnation that we may "behold the glory of God…" (II Corinthians 4:6).[134]

Before I move on further, a clarification must be made here. According to the Divine Economy, deification is not just the redemption of humanity and it is not just the restoration from sin. Rather, it is the crowning of creation, the fulfillment of the whole cosmos. When we lose our identity as mankind, which is belonging to Christ, becoming one with Christ, we forfeit our humanity. As a result, we confine ourselves to the plan of salvation, giving us a narrow view of the Economy of God.[135] The plan of salvation is

---

[131] "Cyril of Alexandria, Commentary on John, LFC 43, 48 (1874/1885). Book 11. Vol. 2 Pp. 453-588.," accessed October 29, 2020, http://www.tertullian.org/fathers/cyril_on_john_11_book11.htm.
[132] Gregory Nazianzen, "Oration 1," *New Advent*, accessed October 29, 2020, https://www.newadvent.org/fathers/310201.htm.
[133] Robert Louis Wilken, *The Spirit of Early Christian Thought: Seeking the Face of God*, (New Haven: Yale University Press, 2005), 153 - 154.
[134] Gama and Sittser, Ibid., 115.
[135] Gama and Sittser, Ibid., 115.

here denoted as Western theology's belief that Christ came to die on the cross to forgive us our sins. Eastern theology, in contrast, stresses Christ invitation to participate in His life through the Incarnation.[136] We end up living this notion of the plan of salvation by merely committing to attending at our local parish rather than venturing through the path of our personal deification. [137] Michael Gama defines this as through the greater arch and the lower arch respectively, where the former is from Creation to Deification and the latter is the Fall to Redemption.[138] Mankind has a history of forgetting who they are and whom they belong to, as evidenced through reading Scripture. We have forgotten our "first love" (Revelation 2:1) and so forget our true destiny as humanity and oppress our appetite for communion with Christ. Despite our *telos* as humans is our deification, our ministerial mindsets convince us that because there a lack of commitment from the young people in local parishes, more and more programs are needed to lure them in.[139] And again, we fail to recognize that not only the young people, but everyone hungers for participation with the Divine. When we live by the lower arch, we believe our sins are forgiven and that is just it. There is no life of virtue to pursue, there is no progress to become human. And therefore, we do not participate in Christ and in His Divine nature. We simply convince ourselves that our sins are forgiven and we go to live our lives as we please. Gregory of Nazianzus tells us that

---

[136] Ibid, 128.
[137] Ibid, 115.
[138] Ibid.
[139] Ibid, 126.

our innate desire is to return "to the pattern it now longs after."[140] Do the goal of our ministries point us to our deepest longings? Do our ministries give space for such a participation? Are we equipping young people with the knowledge of who they are and to whom they belong?

Culture

If our response to the Incarnate word of God, the Word made flesh, who came into our world and embraced Jewish culture, is *theosis,* then we too must incarnate to the world by the ways of culture. If our Maker imprinted in us His image and formed us for the Kingdom to come through our participation in His Nature, then He invites us on a journey, on a process of molding and transforming. And at the same time, if our postmodern culture is on a journey of its own, seeking its identity and purpose, should we not, as the church, boldly approach those seekers and let them know what and who they are looking for? Our youth seek and long for what the church has inherited. Yet we deprive them of the "pearl of great price" (Matthew 14:36) by trying to increase their mind's information through developing more and more programs, all the while completely failing to hear their crying and anguished souls. The same with the home; we demand of the church that it take full responsibility for the spiritual formation of our young, inadequately seeing our role as the spiritual nurturers of the household. We

---

[140] Gregory of Nazianzus, *On God and Christ: The Five Theological Orations and Two Letters to Cledonius* (Yonkers: St. Vladimir's Press, 2002), 50.

undoubtedly fail our children as they end up not developing the faith of the saints that we eagerly preach. The Cappadocians illustrated for us how essential it is to study the contemporary culture as it teaches us the hearts and minds of its people. By acquiring such knowledge, these Cappadocian men and women were able to use the culture as a conduit for salvation. They learned and used pagan language and thought and Christianized it in order that the people may be able to have a true encounter and a real authentic experience with their Savior.

These great men and women challenge us today, by their way of life, to go and embrace our current culture, to seek out the hearts of those wandering and to bring them out of their own selves and confusion. Done in the right way, we bring to light our culture's desire for identity, authenticity, and encounter in such a flat, cold world. We must educate ourselves with the ways of our children that we may reclaim them for Christ in our homes and local churches and empower them to embrace the struggle of faith in which Jacob, in Genesis 32, encountered through a face-to-face experience with God and that they may know their true identity as the beloved children of God.

In order to reclaim their hearts, we must equip them with the right faith through a ministry of discipleship in our homes and local parishes.

Discipleship

The Church provides us with the image of the divine life, the road map to our humanity, the fulfillment of who we were created to be. This means that all aspects of the church should provide this road map; every ministry, event, retreat, Bible study, and meeting.[141] How does the church manifest such a life to her members? I believe we must go back to the key figures of this study: the Cappadocians.

Apostolic succession has been in the DNA of the Orthodox Church since the beginning. It is the very heartbeat of the Church as it is a living relationship with the Holy Spirit and a communion with the saints. It is a handing down from person to person, from one heart to another;[142] it a spiritual parenting that our hearts long for as it relentlessly seeks role models, manifesting in the way we hold on to stories and make the heroes of these stories our very own models and inspirations. Discipleship is what has preserved our true faith, right worship, and authentic experience.[143] The Cappadocians model for us this same discipleship that we observed over the centuries, which only emphasizes the need and continuation of the same practice today. This ministry of discipleship is a heart to heart, soul to soul ministry, a place where I bring the presence of the Lord to the other. We are both in His presence, seeking His wisdom as our teacher and beloved, here He speaks and here He heals. This is not just a ministry but a life of discipleship which lives out the Trinitarian faith, a harmonious dance towards one another, submitting under each other's feet.[144]

---

[141] Bobrinskoy, Ibid., 124.
[142] Ibid, 154.
[143] Ibid, 153.
[144] Silvas, *Ibid.*, 39.

A picture of discipleship is painted for us today through the Cappadocian Mothers and inevitably the Cappadocian Fathers. The life of virtue they were immersed in translates to us that as

> "we become an image of the image, having achieved the beauty of the Prototype through activity as a kind of imitation, as did Paul, who became an 'imitator of Christ,' through his virtue."[145]

It is through this imitation, as I sit in the presence of my mentor, where Christ is present, I am

> "coming closer to the inaccessible Beauty, [I] have become beautiful, and like a mirror, as it were, [I] have taken on [His] appearance.[146] As I imitate the one guiding me, who imitates Christ, who has gone before me, I knock at the ancient doors (Jeremiah 6:16), and I hear Christ sing to me, 'you have become fair because you have come near to my light, and by this closeness to me you have attracted this participation in beauty.'"[147]

Macrina the Younger embodied this rhythm for her brothers, who were deeply inspired to live a life worthy of their calling. Nyssa saw, through his sister, that we receive within ourselves the likeness of whatever we look upon as

---

[145] St. Gregory of Nyssa, *St. Gregory of Nyssa Ascetical Works*, Virginia Woods Callahan, trans. (Washington, D.C: The Catholic University of America Press, 1999), 58.
[146] Jean Danielou, *From Glory to Glory: Texts from Gregory of Nyssa's Mystical Writings* (Crestwood: St. Vladimir's Seminary Press, 1997), 171.
[147] Ibid, 171.

her spiritual life [shone] within the clarity of [her] soul, as she was constantly gazing towards her Bridegroom.[148]

Are our ministries offering us this pure faith, this true worship, and this real experience?[149] Bobrinskoy suggests that every part of our ministries whether it be pastoral, teaching, or administrative, should participate in this sacramental life of transformation, of Christ being the goal of all.[150] It is through discipleship that the life of Christ is revealed, a life of virtue participating daily in the Divine Nature. As is told by Gregory of Nyssa, who did not see himself as an inventor rather a faithful disciple to his older brother Basil, who built on what he inherited, enabling him to become a key player in the second Ecumenical Council in 381.[151]

The baton was handed down to men of faith through discipleship, which emphasized a handing down of a way of life, resulting in saints translating this way of life into writing. Two major figures played a role in the development of the theology that the church inherited and preserves for us today: Athanasius of Alexandria and Origen of Alexandria. The Cappadocian Fathers, though living in a different region, developed their writings on *theosis* based off of Athanasius' expansion of his Trinitarian language. And in the same way it is evident that despite living in a different

---

[148] Ibid, 172–3.
[149] Ibid, 153.
[150] Ibid, 100.
[151] Brooks Otis, *Cappadocian Thought as a Coherent System* (Cambridge: Harvard University Press, 1958).

era than Origen, these same men, were influenced by Origen through their grandmother, Macrina the Elder.[152] Macrina the Elder brought to her family the Kingdom through her faithfulness and love for Christ by her imitation of Gregory the Wonderworker. She instilled the church in her home and as a result, generations after her followed in participating in the Body of Christ.

Are we living this faith for our children to imitate? Are we true mirrors of the Image? Are our ministries infused with the life of Christ? Are our ministries handing down the way to the Kingdom?

---

[152] Sunberg and Noble, Ibid., 53, 63, 66.

Conclusion

We began this study by identifying who the Cappadocian mothers are: Macrina the Elder, Emmelia, Macrina the Younger, Nonna, and Gorgonia. Macrina the Elder was the grandmother and the reason such faith was transmitted to generations after her. She illustrated to her family a life of holiness and graciousness, a life that pointed to the lover of her soul. In chapter two, we saw how all these women participated in the life of virtue, a life sanctified and immersed in prayer and Scripture. Through their way of being, they became the patterns of mothers, sisters, teachers and wives. Their home was a church, filled with the fragrance of Christ, infusing every person who lived in their household and anyone who entered. Their fragrance nurtured, formed, and transformed their communities. Their aroma lives on today through the writings of the Cappadocian Fathers: Basil the Great, Gregory of Nazianzus, and Gregory of Nyssa, who we are indebted to for many reasons. They became the images of the Image, a mirror of imitation that in turn, shaped Orthodox theology. For these women, theology was a way of living not mere theoretical words and abstracts, like theology can be in our modern day. The Fathers' writings, which became our theology, were based off of lives lived and observed that spoke and revealed the marvelous Light (I Peter 2:9).

Chapter two also emphasized that each person is designed and destined to live in communion with God, *theosis*, a daily participation through the ways of virtue. Man was called to become one with God by cultivating virtue, a way of being, a molding of one's character that allowed man to behold Christ.

The lives of both these Mothers and Fathers demand us today to follow such a path, a path that leads to the true humanity of all. We saw in their example the way they engaged and studied their contemporary culture, which enabled them to be vessels for the Truth. They understood the heart of the culture as they managed a healthy relationship with it and embraced it. The Cappadocians saw the brokenness of their culture and were able to bring the Healer to their people; baptizing it through the language and the mode of culture which was familiar to the people. It is imperative that we learn this approach today.

In chapter three, we acknowledged the imminent framework of Secular2 that our current generation abides by and have continually insisted on giving a wrong solution to our modern-day problem. We currently function as if today's problem is trying to fight off the secular world's force, which is consuming our children's minds with societal conduct. Reactionarily, we want to flood our children with as much information as possible about their faith that they may be able to battle the fierce arguments they encounter in their schools and workplaces. Our homes fail to assume a life of *theosis* as we see our children slipping away from church and so we demand from our local parishes that our children be more engaged. As a response, we continue to add more of the same programs under new and modern titles to entice our young people into the four walls of the church. We bombard them with information and fail to be attentive to their cry for transformation.

We saw in chapter four how the running theme in our Cappadocian Mothers and Fathers' lives is the life of *theosis*, an eternal journey in which one's soul is transformed into the likeness of the God. This mode of existence begins in the home, in the way of imitating and mirroring our life givers, which is interpreted as a ministry of discipleship. Simultaneously, the Church reveals the reality of Him in whom we "live and move and have our being" (Acts 17:28) and gives us the means of carrying out this lifelong endeavor of the unification of man and God. This life is illuminated through discipleship, a heart to heart, soul to soul ministry. A ministry that allows space for the others' brokenness where they are known and loved. A ministry where Christ is the aim and vision who brings true healing to our aching wounds. A ministry that invites us and welcomes us, each by name, to sit at the banquet table of the heavenly Kingdom.

Our challenge today, we ask, do our homes look like the Cappadocian Mothers' homes? Do our ministries at our local parishes have Christ as their goal, the One who fills all in all? May the prayers of those who have finished the race be with us and guide us to a life in Him, Who invites us to His table, to participate in His Divine nature.

Bibliography

Rachel Held Evans. "15 Reasons I Left Church." Accessed September 23, 2020. https://rachelheldevans.com/blog/15-reasons-i-left-church.

"1995.02.02, Mitchell, Anatolia: Land, Men, and Gods in Asia Minor – Bryn Mawr Classical Review." Accessed August 12, 2020. https://bmcr.brynmawr.edu/1995/1995.02.02/.

Acts 17:28, n.d.

Bobrinskoy, Boris. *The Mystery of the Church: A Course in Orthodox Dogmatic Theology*. Yonkers: St. Vladimir's Seminary Press, 2012.

Burrus, Virginia. "Macrina's Tattoo." *Journal of Medieval and Early Modern Studies* 33, no. 3 (September 1, 2003): 403–17. https://doi.org/10.1215/10829636-33-3-403.

Carlson, Kent, Mike Lueken, and Dallas Willard. *Renovation of the Church: What Happens When a Seeker Church Discovers Spiritual Formation*. Downers Grove: IVP Books, 2011.

Barna Group. "Church Dropouts Have Risen to 64%—But What About Those Who Stay?" Accessed December 8, 2020. https://www.barna.com/research/resilient-disciples/.

Clement of Alexandria. "The Paedagogus." *New Advent*. Accessed May 17, 2019. http://www.newadvent.org/fathers/02091.htm.

Cyprian, and Allen Brent. *On the Church: Select Letters*. Crestwood: St. Vladimir's Seminary Press, 2006.

Cyril of Alexandria. "Commentary on John, LFC 43, 48 (1874/1885). Book 11. Vol. 2 Pp. 453-588." Accessed October 29, 2020. http://www.tertullian.org/fathers/cyril_on_john_11_book11.htm.

Daley, Brian. *Gregory of Nazianzus*. London: Routledge, 2006.

Danielou, Jean. *From Glory to Glory: Texts from Gregory of Nyssa's Mystical Writings*. Crestwood: St. Vladimir's Seminary Press, 1997.

Deferrari, Roy J. *Saint Basil: The Letters.* Cambridge: Harvard University, 1961.

Effective Christian Ministry. "Effective Christian Ministry." Accessed September 17, 2020. https://effectivechristianministry.org/.

Ferguson, Marilyn. *The Aquarian Conspiracy: Personal and Social Transformation in Our Time.* New York: TarcherPerigee, 2009.

Frank, Georgia. "Macrina's Scar: Homeric Allusion and Heroic Identity in Gregory of Nyssa's Life of Macrina." *Journal of Early Christian Studies* 8, no. 4 (December 1, 2000): 511–30. https://doi.org/10.1353/earl.2000.0063.

Gama, Michael Paul, and Gerald L. Sittser. *Theosis: Patristic Remedy for Evangelical Yearning at the Close of the Modern Age.* Eugene: Wipf and Stock, 2017.

Gregory Nazianzen. "Oration 1." *New Advent.* Accessed October 29, 2020. https://www.newadvent.org/fathers/310201.htm.

Gregory Nazianzen. "Oration 8." *New Advent.* Accessed July 7, 2020. https://www.newadvent.org/fathers/310208.htm.

Gregory Nazianzen. "Oration 18." *New Advent.* Accessed August 21, 2020. https://www.newadvent.org/fathers/310218.htm.

Gregory Nazianzen. "Oration 43." *New Advent.* Accessed July 4, 2020. https://www.newadvent.org/fathers/310243.htm.

Gregory, Bishop of Nyssa. "The Life of Macrina." *Monastic Matrix.* Accessed July 7, 2020. https://monasticmatrix.osu.edu/cartularium/life-macrina-gregory-bishop-nyssa.

Gregory of Nyssa. *The Life of Saint Macrina.* Translated by Kevin Corrigan. Eugene: Wipf and Stock, 2005.

Gregory of Nyssa. *Saint Gregory of Nyssa Ascetical Works.* Translated by Virginia Woods Callahan. Washington, D.C: The Catholic University of America Press, 1999.

Guroian, Vigen. *Tending the Heart of Virtue: How Classic Stories Awaken a Child's Moral Imagination.* New York: Oxford University Press, 2002.

Harrison, Nonna Verna, Basil, and Verna E. F. Harrison. *On The Human Condition: St Basil the Great*. Crestwood: St. Vladimir's Seminary Press, 2005.

Holy Apostles Convent. *The Lives of the Spiritual Mothers*. Buena Vista: Holy Apostles Convent Publications, 1993.

Liddell, Henry George, Robert Scott, and Roderick McKenzie. *Greek-English Lexicon, Ninth Edition with a Revised Supplement*. Edited by Henry Stuart Jones. Oxford: Clarendon Press, 1996.

McKnight, Scot, and N. T. Wright and Dallas Willard. *The King Jesus Gospel: The Original Good News Revisited*. Grand Rapids: Zondervan Academic, 2016.

NW, 1615 L. St, Suite 800Washington, and DC 20036USA202-419-4300 | Main202-857-8562 | Fax202-419-4372 | Media Inquiries. "More Americans Now Say They're Spiritual but Not Religious." *Pew Research Center* (blog). Accessed September 23, 2020. https://www.pewresearch.org/fact-tank/2017/09/06/more-americans-now-say-theyre-spiritual-but-not-religious/.

NW, 1615 L. St, Suite 800 Washington, and DC 20036 USA202-419-4300 | Main202-419-4349 | Fax202-419-4372 | Media Inquiries. "U.S. Religious Landscape Survey: Religious Beliefs and Practices." *Pew Research Center's Religion & Public Life Project* (blog), June 1, 2008. https://www.pewforum.org/2008/06/01/u-s-religious-landscape-survey-religious-beliefs-and-practices/.

Oden, Thomas C. *After Modernity...What?* Grand Rapids: Zondervan Academic, 1992.

Otis, Brooks. *Cappadocian Thought as a Coherent System*. Cambridge: Harvard University Press, 1958.

Paton, W. R., trans. *The Greek Anthology, Volume II: Book 7: Sepulchral Epigrams. Book 8: The Epigrams of St. Gregory the Theologian*. London: Harvard University Press, 1917.

Recluse, Theophan the, and P. E. Gillquist. *Raising Them Right: A Saint's Advice on Raising Children*. Translated by Hieromonk S. Rose, n.d.

Root, Andrew. *Faith Formation in a Secular Age: Responding to the Church's Obsession with Youthfulness*. Grand Rapids: Baker Academic, 2017.

Schaff, Philip. *Schaff's History of the Christian Church, Volume 1 Apostolic Christianity A.D. 1-100*. Peabody: Hendrickson Publishers, 1996.

Silvas, Anna. *Macrina the Younger: Philosopher of God*. Turnhout: Brepols, 2008.

Smith, James K. A. *How (Not) to Be Secular: Reading Charles Taylor*. Grand Rapids: Eerdmans, 2014.

St. Basil the Great. "Address to Young Men on the Right Use of Greek Literature." Accessed August 28, 2020. http://www.tertullian.org/fathers/basil_litterature01.htm.

St. Basil the Great. "Letter 223." *New Advent*. Accessed August 12, 2020. https://www.newadvent.org/fathers/3202223.htm.

St. Cyprian of Carthage and Allen Brent. *On the Church: Select Treatises*. Crestwood: St. Vladimir's Seminary Press, 2006.

St. Gregory of Nazianzus. *On God and Christ: The Five Theological Orations and Two Letters to Cledonius*. Crestwood: St. Vladimir's Seminary Press, 2002.

"St. Macrina the Elder." *New Advent*. Accessed July 4, 2020. https://www.newadvent.org/cathen/09508b.htm.

St. Nektarios of Pentapolis. *For Mind and Heart: St. Nektarios as Teacher*. Translated by Rev Dr John Palmer. Newrome Press LLC, 2020.

Stark, Rodney. *The Triumph of Faith: Why the World Is More Religious than Ever*. Wilmington: Intercollegiate Studies Institute, 2015.

Sunberg, Carla D., and T. A. Noble. *The Cappadocian Mothers*. Eugene: Wipf and Stock, 2017.

Sweet, Leonard. *Post-Modern Pilgrims: First Century Passion for the 21st Century World*. Nashville: B&H Books, 2000.

Tarnas, Richard. *The Passion of the Western Mind: Understanding the Ideas That Have Shaped Our World View*. New York: Ballantine Books, 1993.

Taylor, Charles. *A Secular Age*. Cambridge: Harvard University Press, 2007.

Wilken, Robert Louis. *The Spirit of Early Christian Thought: Seeking the Face of God*. New Haven: Yale University Press, 2005.

www.ingramcontent.com/pod-product-compliance
Lightning Source LLC
Chambersburg PA
CBHW060541080526
44586CB00012B/814